A TO Z

ERIC METAXAS

Tommy
NELSON

Thomas Nelson, Inc.
Nashville

Published in Nashville, Tennessee, by Tommy Nelson™,
a division of Thomas Nelson, Inc.
Managing Editor: Laura Minchew
Project Manager: Karen Gallini

Designed by Koechel Peterson & Associates
Digital color enhancement by Carolyn Guske

Library of Congress Cataloging-in-Publication Data

Metaxas, Eric.

    The Prince of Egypt : A–Z / Eric Metaxas.
      p.   cm.
    Summary: Each letter of the alphabet is represented
by an illustration and a simple rhyme focusing on some
aspect of the life of Moses.
    ISBN 0-8499-5850-4
    1. Moses (Biblical leader)—Juvenile literature. 2. English
language—Alphabet—Juvenile literature. [1. Moses (Biblical
leader) 2. Alphabet.] I. Title.
BS580.M6M37   1998
222'.109505—dc21   98-38570
[E]   CIP
                                    AC

Printed in the United States of America
98 99 00 01 02 03 QPH 9 8 7 6 5 4 3 2 1

 is for Aaron,
who was Moses' big brother.
That explains why they had
the same father and mother.

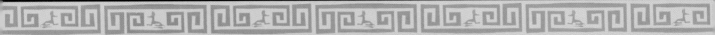

B is for Baby in a Basket,
floating on the river Nile.
Never mind that giant hippo.
Just avoid that crocodile!

C is for the Courage
to do what is right,
as when Moses stood up
to Pharaoh's great might.

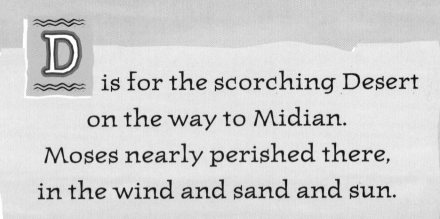

D is for the scorching Desert
on the way to Midian.
Moses nearly perished there,
in the wind and sand and sun.

E is for the Egyptian army, Pharaoh's forces giving chase. When they rode into the sea, they disappeared without a trace.

F is for Faith.
Those who trusted the Lord
had heaven-sent wonders
for their happy reward.

G is for God
at the burning bush.
A fiery voice,
an awesome sound.
Moses trembled
when he heard God say,
"You're standing
on holy ground!"

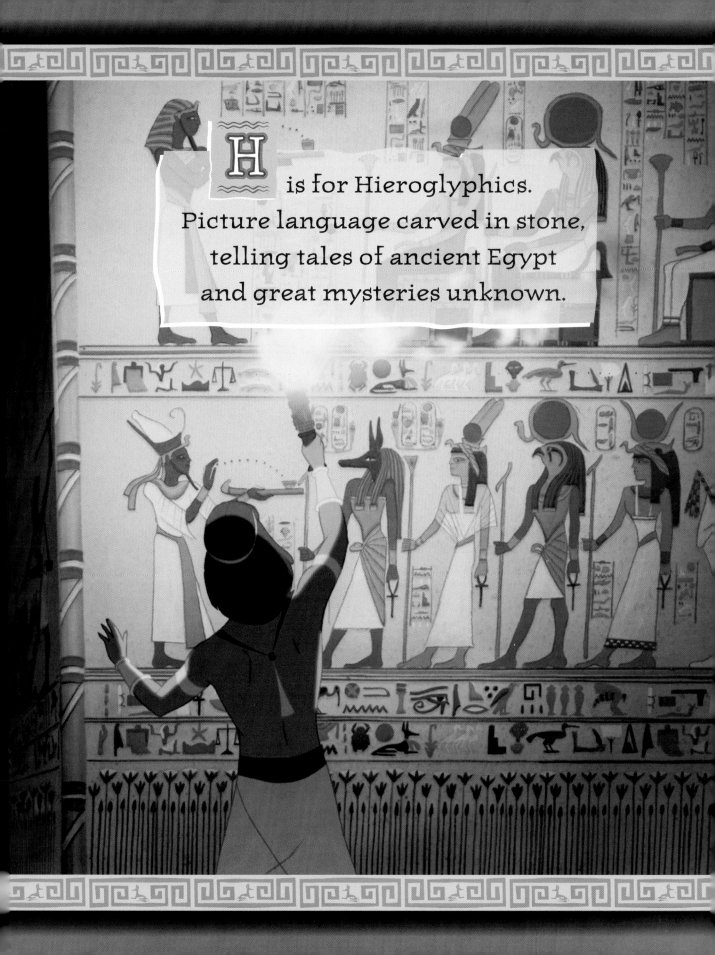

H is for Hieroglyphics.
Picture language carved in stone,
telling tales of ancient Egypt
and great mysteries unknown.

I is for the Israelites,
who wore the yoke of slavery.
But God in heaven heard their cry
and led them out to liberty.

J is for Jethro,
a Midianite priest.
When Moses saved his daughters,
Jethro threw a great feast.

K is for the King of Egypt. Rameses was this Pharaoh's name. By defying God and Moses, he brought himself eternal shame.

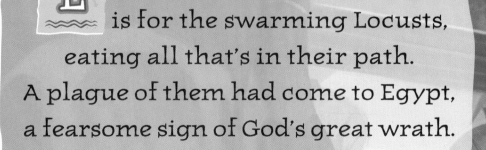

L is for the swarming Locusts,
eating all that's in their path.
A plague of them had come to Egypt,
a fearsome sign of God's great wrath.

is for Miriam, Yocheved's daughter. She rejoiced to see Moses plucked out of the water.

N is for the river Nile.
Behold, it's flowing red with blood!
A plague has come upon the land,
a catastrophic crimson flood.

O is for Obedience.
It's right to heed
the Lord's command.
When the Pharaoh disobeyed,
ten awful plagues
swept through the land.

P is for the royal Palace.
Moses lived there as a youth,
thinking Pharaoh was his father,
till at last he learned the truth.

is for the eerie Quiet,
when the plague of darkness came.
Three days long, no golden sun,
not even lights of candle flame.

R is for the great Red Sea.
Moses lifted up his staff.
Behold! A miracle of God!
It parted to reveal a path!

S is for Straw,
which the Hebrews would mix
with water and mud
when making their bricks.

is for the
Ten Commandments,
searing words from
Heaven's Throne,
written with
the Lord's own finger
on two tablets
made of stone.

U is for Unleavened bread.
There was no time to let it rise.
The Hebrews had to leave that night,
so God asked them to improvise.

V is for the Victory
won without a spear or sword.
When you fight for righteousness,
the battle belongs to the Lord.

W is for
the Wedding
in the tents of Midian.
When Tzipporah
married Moses,
life for them
had just begun.

X is for the Exodus,
the Hebrews' flight from slavery.
Sing hallelujah! Shout for joy!
For God had set them free!

Y is for Yocheved,
who was Moses' real mother.
That makes Miriam and Aaron
his sister and brother!

Z is for Tzipporah,
spelled with a "T."
Although when you
pronounce it,
it sounds like a "Z"!